Duluth
Zenith City & Beyond

by
Jan Chronister

Duluth: Zenith City & Beyond
copyright © 2023 by Jan Chronister

All rights reserved.

Except for quotations and excerpts appearing in reviews, this work may not be reproduced or transmitted, in whole or in part, by any means whatsoever, without prior written permission from the author.

ISBN: 978-1-886895-40-9

An imprint of Poetry Harbor

Cover photo by Jan Chronister

Copies of this book are available at amazon.com
or from the author at whispertreepress@gmail.com

Town Life

Urban Renewal *9*
Corn Story *10*
Homeless *11*
Nature Abhors a Vacuum *12*
Bag Boy *13*
Karma *14*
Whole Foods Checkout on Mother's Day *15*
You Don't Need to Pick Lilacs in Duluth *16*
June Wedding, St. Scholastica *17*
Sanctuary *18*
Visiting Tweed *19*
Interrupted Dream *20*
Break a Leg *21*
Summer Stock *22*
Zenith City All Dressed Up *23*
Painting the Town *24*
Wrong Turn *25*
Oil Change *26*
An Unnamed Restaurant in an Unnamed Town *27*
The Physician Attends a Poetry Group *28*
Lynching *29*
Superior Street Revisited *30*
At the Armory *31*
Showhorses *32*
Miller Hill Mall 2050 *33*

Almanac

January Morning *37*
Golden Delicious *38*
Hope *39*
Biography of a Blossom *40*
Valentine's Day *41*
Winter Dream *42*
Whatever Is Lost *43*

Signs of Spring *44*
The Plot against Juhannus Juhlat *45*
Trilliums *46*
Opening Night *47*
Strawberry Moon *48*
August Flood *49*
They made a lot of hay today. . . *50*
Tenth Month *51*
Out of Season *52*
All That Remains *53*
10 November 1975 *54*
Shared Air *55*

Waterways

Winter Hike *59*
Finding Our Way *60*
Hidden Stuff *61*
Keeping Secrets *62*
Below Thomson Dam on Good Friday *63*
Spring Cleaning *64*
Estuary *65*
Chasing Waterfalls *66*
Back North *67*
Voyageurs *68*
Beach Confession *69*
Lake Superior Blue *70*
Duluth Gets Her Day in the Sun (Almost) *71*

Roads

The Summer We Bought the Farm *75*
South of Forbes *76*
For Katie *77*
At St. Mary's after the Accident *78*
Commute *79*
Morning Meal *80*

Roadkill *81*
White Crosses *82*
Descent *83*
The Effect of Sleeping Children *84*
In the Doorway *85*
Detour *86*
Lodestone *87*

Notes from the Author *88*
Acknowledgments *90*
About the Author *93*

Town Life

Experience is one thing you can't get for nothing.
~Oscar Wilde

Urban Renewal

In a certain year
all the wooden stairs downtown
must have been painted
by the same man.

I can see him now,
armed with what he thinks will bring
a touch of forest to the streets.
Cleaning away silt, litter, ash,
he coats the worn steps
with floor and deck enamel,
John Deere Green.

In a few days
the gloss is gone.
Powdery footprints,
ring marks from bottles,
butts of hand-rolled cigarettes
paint portraits
of the unseen.

Corn Story

I walk into the mission on First Street,
drop produce in a dark room.
Corn, tomatoes, squash, peppers glow
like gems encrusted on a crucifix.

People huddle on the sidewalk,
lives reduced to backpacks.
Inside at crowded tables
they eat kernels filled
with memories of sun.

Homeless

At 36 she looks
so much older
in the newspaper photo—
dark circles under her eyes,
cold sore on her lip—
but what woman wouldn't,
living in a tent in the woods
above Duluth.

It's 34 this morning,
next week looks worse.
Only the homeless
and recreationalists
stay outdoors much longer.

Now that police
have cleared out the camp,
a reporter asks what's next.
She is quoted: "I'm just going to move
to a different spot."

Nature Abhors a Vacuum

I ask about you
at the powwow,
find out you died.
Did I speak your name too soon?

I learn of another
who danced with death,
refuse to say his name.
Instead I call him
Fagan, a role he played on stage,
a man who taught homeless boys
to fill their empty pockets.

Bag Boy

He lives on a dairy farm
outside of town,
never went to college
'cause the cows were always there.

Arms laced with paper scratches,
fingers pinched by canned goods,
the underpaid bag boy
smiles at shoppers,
reads want ads
on his break.

Karma

After checking myself out at Walmart
I notice the small box of face cream
in the corner of my cart.

I could have kept it when I got to my car,
made away with something for nothing,
thought about the theft every night when
smoothing my face.

I go back through the checkout, pay $9.99
plus tax, drive home through green lights,
sleep with a clean conscience,
never write the other poem.

Whole Foods Checkout on Mother's Day

In front of me
a father and son
buy a greeting card.
I forget what day it is
because my mother is gone.

Across the aisle
wrapped bouquets smile.
Father sends boy to grab one.
It scans at $14.99.

In six words he tells his son
what mothers are worth—
"Put it back,
that's too much."

I should have given him
the fifteen bucks.

You Don't Need to Pick Lilacs in Duluth

The whole city becomes a bowl
filled with fragrance
overpowering paper mills and dog smells.

Exploding bushes cast their hue
on buildings—
sandstone turns violet,
clapboards become amethyst—
the air a distillery of their scent.

June Wedding, St. Scholastica

Red and white tulips gossip,
dandelion heads wait for wedding to end.

Bridal couple appears,
blessed with perfect weather.
Framed by sanctuary entrance,
they gaze out the door
at their new life,
dodge handfuls of rice
thrown for good fortune.

Reception follows,
requisite speeches,
endless photos,
food and dance.

Suited man with boutonnière
heads to parking lot
keys in hand,
anxious to go out for a beer.

Sun disappears behind clouds,
coolness sharpens
the fleeting perfection
of marriage.

Sanctuary

Over a bridge
a castle high sits on the hill.
Crenellated towers hold it down.

Near the roofline
of the chapel
saints in niches scold,
pigeon spikes shimmer.

Chips of quartz, mica
glimmer like ice.
Pots of red geraniums
mark rooms of retired nuns.

Copper weathervane—
small ship with two masts—
points south
away from frigid water
to the last building,
assisted living for those
who need help in their last days.
Overhead, angel clouds float.

Visiting Tweed

Docent points at paintings
(landscapes, he says).
Images resemble snipped threads
on a rug, bag of leftover yarn,
look more like exotic food
than sky and field.

Upstairs, black and white photographs
record the mundane,
endow meaning to what eyes can see.

Interrupted Dream

We're in an Alumna Craft
puttering up the Brule
with a five-horse motor,
three poets and me.
We ride tracks
with trains overtaking us,
duck and emerge
shook up but intact.

I'm running around UMD
with laundry,
same three poets
wait in the car.
I finally come out,
realize I left
my basket behind,
decide it's too embarrassing
to go back where
a faculty meeting
is taking place.

I wake up craving those doughnuts
that come in a windowed box.
My husband says I could
probably get some at that
new dollar store out on the highway.
Maybe I'll buy a laundry basket too.

Break a Leg

"It's a wonderful cast," the director said.

I thought he was referring to the
plaster worn by the leading lady
after her fall off the stage.

During the blackout for curtain call,
dressed as a nun, she tripped
on her tent of dark cloth.

Her reactions may be a bit slow tonight,
movements laced with pain,
but the show must go on
broken leg and all.

Summer Stock

Costumes hang in dark theatre,
wait to bloom on stage.
Exotic perennials of purple velvet
blue brocade
flower for a few brief weeks,
glow in spotlights
adorning, adored,
then packed up and stored
for next summer.

Zenith City All Dressed Up

Mesabi bodice
pinned with towers,
sequins of topaz street lights,
beach bracelets
lace bridges
encircled by blue velvet skirt.

Painting the Town

Back in 1996
the *Duluth News Tribune*
brought in a newspaper designer
from Miami.
She spent time
driving around
taking in the sights,
returned to the office,
got to work,
came up with a palette
suited to Duluth:
Oreboat Red
Superior Blue
Lift Bridge Gray

They could have just asked
the people who worked there.

Wrong Turn

At the loading dock of the newspaper plant
I encounter a truck driver.
He looks lost.
"Can I help you?" I ask.
"I'm here to deliver paper to the *Duluth Tribune*,"
he says with a definite drawl.
"Duluth, Minnesota?" I ask.
"Aw sheet!" he says, pronouncing
sheet like a two-syllable word.
"Were you supposed to go to Duluth, Georgia?"
"Aw sheet!"

Oil Change

Every 3000 miles I pull into Harwell's
where they still patch tires and fix old cars.
John the mechanic is a short, bright-eyed
Santa Claus kind of guy. His brother Jim
lives behind the garage in what was
their father's house when the station
glowed under a neon Pegasus.

Jim hides out in the oil change pit
pouring his own 100 proof version
of 10W 30. John works
on my car fast and cheap,
one eye on his brother.

An Unnamed Restaurant in an Unnamed Town

Just before the noon rush
our waitress hugs a man as he leaves,
hands him money.
I'm thinking she owes him
or he's selling stuff.

I wait outside the ladies room.
She stays in there a long time,
comes out sniffling. My mind
runs in the direction of drugs,
but who am I to judge
with my morning coffee
and evening wine? Could be
a sick child, late rent.

When the lunch crowd
hits its peak, so does she—
moving fast, full of smiles.

The Physician Attends a Poetry Group

It's a discussion of Ocean Vuong.
How he creates new mythology with
animals & colors & bodies.
How a father, piano, lovers
provide a retreat. How he repeats on purpose so
we know what's important.

Red, white & blue sing of
violence, women, death.
Mouths & shoulders & eyes
open holes of escape.
Animals know what
humans only guess at.

The doctor touches exit wounds
made by grenades, hunters in fields.
Rain falls too hard, bruises bodies.
A horse follows a blue path
home to the stars.

Lynching

Elias, Elmer, and Isaac
were like other nineteen-year-old boys
when the Twenties started to roar.
Working hard, playing hard
trying to stay out of trouble.

One June night
a girl cried rape
and Elias, Elmer, and Isaac
found themselves in jail.

One-tenth of the city's citizens
turned out to join the mob. The fact
that the girl had a reputation
didn't mean a thing. That the boys
were being framed
never entered angry heads.

Black men had raped a white girl
was all they needed to know.
Before Justice could cover her eyes
Elias, Elmer, and Isaac were dead.

Superior Street Revisited

Through the open window
two blocks up the hill
Abram Zimmerman
hears the jeers, cheers
of the mob at night
as the jail doors break
and three young blacks
hang from a lamp post
in downtown Duluth.

A crowd surrounds,
pictures taken,
postcards made.

It's 1920; he's eight years old,
is told he's lucky
to be in America,
not somewhere else.

At the Armory

The figure on stage
in suit, tie and white shirt
takes his music seriously,
croons a love song to Peggy Sue.

Three days later
an after-concert flight to Fargo
crashes, killing all on board.

They called it the day the music died
but a seventeen-year-old in the audience
proved them wrong.

Showhorses

Three high school girls
run up the hill
spotlighted by five-o'clock sun,
ponytails swaying.

One hundred years ago
Buffalo Bill might have stood
at Codyview's front window
and smiled.

Miller Hill Mall 2050

I have dreams about the mall
reverting back to nature
like an abandoned farmstead.

Deer wander in and out of stores,
punctuate carpets with their sophisticated tracks,
shiny pellets.

Wind blows through
open doors in Sears,
curled brown leaves
race in circles,
mingle with receipts,
foam cups.

Squirrels nest in skylights,
worms and frogs
set up house in fountains.

Trout swim in Miller Creek,
the temperature perfect
now that runoff is clean
and trees shade its banks.

In time,
concrete disappears,
the corner is crowned with tansy and birch.

Almanac

To be interested in the changing seasons is a happier state of mind than to be hopelessly in love with spring.
~George Santayana

January Morning

Fifteen below is normal
this time of year
but it still reaches some deep part
of my soul, reminds me
how fragile it all really is.

I open the bedroom blinds.
Each pane wears a layer of ice
that starts to weep
when warm air hits it.

Outside blue jays sit
on branches, look in.
When I feed them,
the cold fear
that wraps my heart
thaws.

Golden Delicious

It's January
boots in school hall.
I pull an apple
from my lunch bag.

I see our tree
obscured by blossoms in spring,
courting pollinators.
During summer visits
thistles pierce bare feet.
In August I examine hard green balls,
festoon my pants with burrs.
Leaves fall, first snow
frosts each gold orb.

We fill bushels,
leave the rest for deer.
They come at night,
stretch high like dancers,
eat warm sun
buried deep within
cold fruit.

Hope

After sliding through January
February seems endless.
Snow inches past bird baths,
buries the mailbox.
On the windowsill
pepper seeds sprout,
cotyledons emerge,
unfold green wings
that will fly us to spring.

Biography of a Blossom

Each morning I cut up
an apple to take to school
not from a backyard tree
but New Zealand hills
soft with pink
where our winter snow
is summer dust.

Lobed fruits
travel to Duluth
in dark holds of ships,
unload like coal,
truck to the grocer,
line up like valentines from the sun.

Valentine's Day

Across the lake
Two Harbors shines sharp in cold air,
breakwater lighthouse beckons,
flashy ring on a slowly turning finger
in the jeweler's showcase.

In February
the days are finally
long enough
to take a walk after work.
I think of deer in the woods
chest deep in snow
eating twigs.

Some people feed them,
save them to stalk later,
like abusive partners
bearing gifts.

Winter Dream

Orion wades over the horizon,
tromps on the tiara
of far-away Duluth.
A white spider
weaves a frozen web across
my February calendar.
He barely finishes
when the warm hand of March
turns the page, sends splinters
of icy silk against the wall.
Crystals melt into small pools I step in
when I get out of bed.

Whatever Is Lost

In winter we lose
the desire to look too far
beyond dusk,
sit in circles of white light.

Our souls startle
at the old cat's spine
poking through thinning fur,
the gray in our son's hair,
how fast a tumor grows.

On frigid afternoons
we open mailboxes,
find letters of loss,
watch the sun float north.

A few weeks before
Easter we surprise ourselves
when light pours into
upstairs rooms,
recovers what was lost.

Signs of Spring

April 5, 2:21 p.m.
the first saltie arrives
in Duluth's Harbor.

It's been a long winter
as it always is.
Snow-blanket lies tattered,
streets pitted with holes.
Flowerpots appear on porches.
We find all the things
we forgot to bring
in last October.

The Plot against Juhannus Juhlat

Less than two months shy of solstice
snow covers the ground,
glowing in late daylight
like clean sheets.
Ice laces evergreen gowns
just in time for high school proms.

One more storm,
one last slippery road.
In my car I play the blues,
there's nothing else to do.

Trilliums

First white of spring
glows in the woods,
constellations light up the dark,
damp forest floor
fills with stars

Opening Night

Cowslips in ditches
ready to bloom,
crisp new currency of Spring.

Amphibians jam,
frogs tune up
on fern French horns.

Slim glimmer of moon,
edge of silver sequin
on evening's gown.

Stage curtained
with Northern Lights,
a limited engagement.

Strawberry Moon

I spend the morning
peeling open folded
strawberry leaves
like the pages
of a water-soaked book.
I look for leaf rollers—
yellow-green larvae
that plague our beds this year.
Small green fruits become black craters.

I set out leggy zinnias, stake a few
against the strong south wind.
Visions of last summer's
plate-size blooms feed my faith.

At night, I curl up in bed,
caterpillar in cocoon,
dream of harvest beyond
June's full moon.

August Flood

After weeks of rain and mud, the sun comes out
burning away rust, mold, sadness.
Sheet rock crumbles like wet chalk.
Rescued tomatoes glow like rubies.
The cat we thought was dead jumps down
from the second floor.
We shovel out brown soup,
use up bottles of bleach,
salvage what we can of summer.

They made a lot of hay today...

started as soon as the dew dried,
worked by headlights until ten;
clover dust rising like smoke.

They left giant round biscuits
that will fill winter barns with sweetness
while cows breathe manhole steam
out their slick, black nostrils.

When September ends I realize
the sun is too low to matter,
garden almost dead.
I dream of purple clover,
intoxicating scent
buried in bales of hay.

Tenth Month

Final barefoot days,
lawn layered in leaves.
They dance in circles at midnight,
lock their curled edges together in a thick crust,
cast a spell, bewitch us
so we can't see Orion's belt
hanging on the hook.

Out of Season

Snow slides off
still-green leaves
of lilacs and peonies.
Yesterday's robust
marigolds wear
stocking hats.

We saw the forecast,
figured fifty-percent chance
would happen somewhere else.

Two weeks before
the legendary blizzard of '91
we get a taste of what's ahead.

All That Remains

abandoned
stalks of corn
forgotten

ragged men
with their backs
to the wind

burnished oaks
drained of wine
wait for spring

10 November 1975

Last century's mythical waves
rise, ready to snake-swallow ships.
Innocent sailors sleep like mice
in freighter's cave, her name
forever linked with disaster.

Shared Air

I sit outside
two days from solstice,
breathe in, out, see puffs of breath,
remember being a kid.
We built snow castles,
never felt cold hands or feet,
just the pure joy of fresh air.

In the giant hemlock that guards our yard
chickadees fluff feathers, prepare for sleep.
I wish I could keep my door open, invite them in,
cast birdseed on the rug.

At night I envision fairy tale forests
where birds alight on a young woman's hand,
tell stories of life in the sky,
how snow is born,
where dreams go.

Waterways

If there is magic on this planet, it is contained in water."
~Loren Eiseley

Winter Hike

Snowshoes plod up frozen North Shore stream,
end of extended January thaw.
Weak tea water heads for Lake Superior,
burbles beneath ice
mostly sealed and white.
Winter regathers herself,
fresh snow becomes canvas for deer tracks,
raven wing-prints.

Finding Our Way

Brown leaf
stuck on river ice
reminds us
of death, decay.

Green stem
in a frozen bubble
sings of thaw,
warmer days.

Hidden Stuff

Everything is made of one hidden stuff.
    ~Ralph Waldo Emerson

Just once I'd like to have a day
to do nothing but watch hawks
and treetop eagles.

Stand by a river when winter melts
and Spring flexes her muscles,
the Embarrass or Temperance
would do just fine.

Feel the weight of frozen months
rise with the boiling sap steam,
my feet once more anchored
to brown, soft ground,
soup stock where ancient elements swim,
hidden stuff of Emerson.

Keeping Secrets

Spring runoff thunders under the road
frothy with foam.
It flows from quiet places
in the hills where spirits gather,
roars with stories told on winter nights,
runs to Lake Superior.

By June only a murmur
of thin wet ribbon ties
high places to the shoreline.

I hear secrets, keep them frozen,
knowing what torrents
would flow if I thawed.

Below Thomson Dam on Good Friday

I am a buoy in the river,
my cable tied to
ancient Laurentian rock.
I hang on tight,
fight the current.

To someone standing on the bridge
I must look useless,
but come back in August
when levels are low
and I will once more
mark safe passage.

Spring Cleaning

Late May,
feather-soft breezes
dust leaves.

Apple blossoms
mop up
winter's clouds.

Lake Superior
is pristine crystal,
polished silver on lace,
a waxed floor
reaching the horizon.

Estuary

morning condensation
on the window
forms the shape of Lake Superior

wolf snout
arched back
island eye

body of water
between us and Canada
summer cooler
winter curse

when it rains
river mouths bleed
from ancient clay beds
laid before worlds
began to explode
before drought
mercury in fish
before moisture on my window
runs like a tear to the sea

Chasing Waterfalls

My sister won't be planting pansies
this spring, replacing them with
impatiens in May.

She won't be taking trips
to Glacier or Tettegouche,
sturdy legs hiking on
rocky trails. When I saw

her last, eyes still bright,
it was eating her up. She could
feel it move through her body,
a predator bound to win.

At the memorial service, a photo shows
her smiling in front of falls.
I say it's Gooseberry,
my brother says
somewhere in Canada.

It doesn't matter.
Air charged with ions
purified her blood,
kept wolves at bay
for a few more months.

Back North

Leaving Georgia's tidal basins,
stagnant swamps where we
struggled to breathe,
we return to cascading bronze ribbons
studded with crystal.
Cloquet and Whiteface rivers
scour their beds, shake out ferns
refresh the air,
leave us
breathless.

Voyageurs

They come from Montreal
in canoes built for twelve,
wear bright hats, sing their songs,
carry loads on strong French Canadian backs,
stop at Michilimackinac,
Sault Ste. Marie,
Grand Portage.

At La Pointe they feast on meals of wild rice,
maple syrup, venison.
Some stay long enough to be counted, some move on,
winter where fur-bearers abound,
return for rendezvous.

Visitors come from St. Paul,
Milwaukee, Chicago,
paddle kayaks to sea caves,
ride the ferry,
take an island cruise.

They carry cameras,
water bottles, brochures,
eat fresh whitefish, apple pie
and ice cream,
go back to their cities
minds full of blue and green.

Beach Confession

Forgive me Mother for I have sinned. . .

I come now, repentant, listening:
clinking of stone currency
offered up for collection,
familiar rustle of hymnal waves.

Beer bottles once broken on deck
are worn smooth like rosary beads
between fingers.

I find teacup handles, plate edges
washed up on shore,
remnants of some ship's
civilization heaved and cracked
by your wrath.

We forget what water can do
until brought to our knees by
hurricanes, baptized by floods.

Lake Superior Blue

If I took a photo
to the paint store,
matched the lake with
one of their chips,
what would the name
turn out to be?

Something frivolous
like *Navy Satin*, *Fresh Hyacinth*,
Crisp French Blue?
Some sparkling shade
like *Bright Sailing*,
Periwinkle, or *Sapphire*?

Chemicals can't
replicate a body of water
that breathes snow,
creates icy hues
on the horizon.

There is no other way
to describe what is simply
Lake Superior Blue.

Duluth Gets Her Day in the Sun (Almost)

Ken Jennings
reveals the Final Jeopardy answer:
"This city of approximately 90,000
is located on the largest lake
in North America."

While the music plays,
my husband and I
scream the answer.

One contestant writes
"What is Minneapolis?"
Second player,
along with the champion,
guess Green Bay.

We groan.
Even Jennings seems mystified
by their mistakes.

Is Duluth so unknown?
True, winters are tests
of survival, summers
short and fleeting,
but surely word of her stark beauty,
stunning presence of Lake Superior,
are enough to earn fame.

We take comfort
in this oversight,
enjoy our Great Lake.

Roads

Still round the corner there may wait
A new road or a secret gate,
And though we pass them by today,
Tomorrow we may come this way
And take the hidden paths that run
Toward the Moon or to the Sun.
~J.R.R. Tolkein

The Summer We Bought the Farm

With a map of Minnesota
and some real estate listings,
we set off from our Milwaukee flat
with a car not really road-safe
but big enough to sleep in.

We take the route through Brainerd
then Bemidji, Paul Bunyan looming,
up to hazy International Falls
where we don't stop, scared off
by belching smokestacks.

Down to Duluth
over the bridge to Wisconsin
we find it—
40 acres, trout stream, artesian well,
house barely livable.
We move right in.

South of Forbes

Between Alborn's soft sofa and the rigid Iron Range
a comb-straight road with even teeth
of tamarack and cedar
pulled immigrants north to boomtowns.

The only current now is water flowing south.
Junked recliner sits
half-submerged in a swamp
like a pharaoh's flooded throne.

For Katie

Through my windshield
a forget-me-not blue sky appears
after weeks of wicked weather.
Approaching Moose Lake
it turns chilly and I shiver.

It was here that bright-eyed Katie
working late at her second job
was abducted by evil.

Her parents' faces plead
on the news.
Those of us with daughters
can only imagine the pain.
With each story her brother's
eyes grow harder as he realizes
what is lost:
sister
secret keeper
teller of tales
friend
daughter
aunt
future wife and mother
nieces and nephews

The Moose Lake exit sign looms over
the freeway, its arrow
curved like a fishhook
as if bent by the will of a thousand minds
with one goal—
catch him.

At St. Mary's after the Accident
for Dagny

IV drips,
slowly dispensing clear fluid
through angel-shaped pouches
and tubes.

Outside,
Lake Superior waves writhe
like bodies in a painting by Bosch.

My x-rays are clear and strong,
ribs sweeping out from
a Viking ship's prow.

Yours are cloudy and broken,
like the windshield of the car
we rode in,
collided at 65 miles per hour.

You lie silent and still,
an old vessel in dry dock,
waiting for repairs.

Commute

Eagle tears gutted cathedral of dry deer ribs.
Tires chant as I drive on labyrinth pavement,
take me home repeating a prayer.

Morning Meal

Sleek crows
line roadsides
like black-suited men
at a breakfast counter
waiting for traffic to clear
so they can get down to business.

My mind is filled
with calendars and caffeine,
mouth tearing a bagel.

A bird flies up, hits my windshield.
I'm going too fast to react
but slow enough to hear wing bones crack,
a quiet universal gasp
before the dark swallowing of death.

Roadkill

Slant of November sun
highlights dead pheasant,
copper red stops my breath—
beauty in death.

White Crosses

They stand stiffly along highways,
bookmarks in pages of miles
urging us to read
their stories.

A Wisconsin groom
leaves his bachelor party
relieves himself in the road,
is struck and killed by his best man's truck.

High school boys
ride with clattering cans,
collide with a train,
leave behind two teams
each one man short.

Descent

I drive down Spirit Mountain in December,
Duluth glows like a Christmas tree.
Beyond the black garland of river
Wisconsin constellations shine—
grid of street lamps,
insistent lights of refinery,
oasis of university.
Above me, towers on the antennae farm
glimmer like old-fashioned hatpins.

I recall a Native woman,
remember she was last seen on that hill
but the details escape me.
Was she getting into a car?
Were some clothes left behind?

She was never found,
name added to the long list
of Missing Murdered Indigenous Women.
Lights turned off too soon.

The Effect of Sleeping Children

Exploding white chrysanthemums,
fireworks of falling snow
seen through the windshield
at fifty-five miles per hour
comes close to hypnosis.

In the back seat
our sleeping children trust us
with surveillance of storms,
conquering cold,
fighting fire.

We feed them our profits,
keep projects closeted,
cultivate patience
and pay the bills.

Sleeping children keep us
from drinking daydreams,
from hypnotic bombardments of light.

In the Doorway

Pocketing his keys he hesitates,
cowboy boots on edge
of ragged linoleum map to nowhere.
Low ceiling wears a necklace of Christmas lights.

She's there—
slouch of recognition
topped with sprayed hair
and mascara.
Her silent language
drowns out TV, traffic,
conversation of afternoon patrons.

Only the bartender reads
the road signs to trouble.

Detour

Late winter in Brookston,
drain pipe ice an old man's beard,
frozen river a rim
on white china plate.

Blindfolded banks
and recycled churches
line bleak streets,
a dying town's dowry.

Jagged foundation
of torn-down school
sits like a ring
without a stone.

Lodestone

On the way up the hill
there's a piece of white
embedded in blacktop.
Remnant, perhaps,
from a porcelain cup,
polished stone, beach
shell. For years
I've used it to mark
my turnaround spot
where I face north,
view Lake Superior
sometimes lost in fog,
sometimes an icy blue strip,
wolf's snout on the map.

Sun pierces clouds,
shines on hills across the lake
where someone walks,
gazes across cold water,
breathes deep.

NOTES FROM THE AUTHOR
(page numbers of poems in parentheses)

(12) "Nature Abhors a Vacuum": Kevin Walsh played Fagan in the Duluth Playhouse production of *Oliver!* Kevin passed away from cancer in 2019. In addition to being an accomplished actor and singer, he was a PA and clinic coordinator for the Fond du Lac Band of Chippewa and medical provider for the CHUM homeless shelter.

(21, 22) "Break a Leg" and "Summer Stock" were inspired by the six years I spent as costume shop manager at the Duluth Playhouse.

(30) "Superior Street Revisited": Abram Zimmerman is Bob Dylan's father. Abram's parents emigrated from Odessa to escape pogroms against Jews. The story of the lynching was reportedly told to a young Robert Zimmerman by his father and is mentioned in Dylan's "Desolation Row." (from the *Wikipedia* article "Bob Dylan")

(31) "At the Armory" references the February 3, 1959 plane crash that killed Buddy Holly, Richie Valens and "The Big Bopper" J. P. Richardson. (from the *Wikipedia* article "Buddy Holly")

(32) "Showhorses": Buffalo Bill Cody lived in Codyview as its owner for sixteen years. It was originally built for his sister Nellie and her husband in 1897-98 on North 77th Avenue West. (from *Northern Wilds* magazine Aug.-Sept. 2012)

(45) "Juhannus Juhlat" is the Finnish Midsummer Festival still celebrated, among other places, at the Oulu Cultural & Heritage Center outside of Iron River, Wisconsin, across the road from where the author lived for six years.

(52) "Out of Season": The Halloween Blizzard of 1991 dumped over three feet of snow in the Duluth area and shut the city down for days.

(53) "All That Remains" is a poetic form known as a tricube.

(54) *The Edmund Fitzgerald* sank in Lake Superior on November 10, 1975 with the loss of the entire crew of 29 men.

(59) "Winter Hike" is an erasure poem using Sam Cook's column in the *Duluth News Tribune* that ran in February 2017 and is used with permission.

(77) "For Katie" is dedicated to Katie Poirer who was abducted and murdered by Donald Blom in 1999.

(78) "At St. Mary's after the Accident": Dagny Bohlin died three days after this poem was written, one month before her 86th birthday.

ACKNOWLEDGMENTS

Many thanks to the editors of the following publications where these poems have previously appeared, some in slightly different versions:

"All That Remains." *Highland Park Poetry*, 2019.

"At St. Mary's after the Accident." *Dust&Fire*, 2000.

"At the Armory." *Visiting Bob* (New Rivers Press, 2018).

"August Flood." *Weatherbeaten Lit*, 2017.

"Beach Confession." *Wrath: Seven Deadly Sins Vol. 5* (Pure Slush Books, 2018).

"Biography of a Blossom." *Peacock Journal*, 2018.

"Chasing Waterfalls." *The Thunderbird Review*, 2020.

"Corn Story." *Empty Shoes Anthology*, 2009.

"Estuary." *Wisconsin Poets' Calendar*, 2017.

"Golden Delicious." *Sky Island Journal*, 2017.

"Hidden Stuff." *Mother Superior*, 1996.

"Homeless." *Home* (Pure Slush, 2023).

"Hope." *New Beginnings* (Stacy Savage, 2020).

"In the Doorway." *Of Burgers & Barrooms* (Main Street Rag, 2017).

"Interrupted Dream." *The Nemadji Review*, 2023.

"January Morning." *The Wild Word*, 2022.

"Karma." *The Nemadji Review*, 2021.

"Lake Superior Blue." *Last Stanza Poetry Journal #9*, 2022.

"Lodestone." *Red Cedar*, 2021.

"Morning Meal." *Dust&Fire*, 2003.

"Nature Abhors a Vacuum." *The Thunderbird Review*, 2021.

"10 November 1975." *Decennia* (Truth Serum Books, 2019).

"Opening Night." *North Coast Review*, 1993.

"Out of Season." *Flight Patterns* (Poetry Harbor, 2022).

"Shared Air." *Flight Patterns* (Poetry Harbor, 2022).

"Spring Cleaning." *Caught Between Coasts* (Clover Valley Press, 2018).

"Strawberry Moon." *Highland Park Poetry*, 2023.

"Summer Stock." *Summer* (Pure Slush, 2016).

"Tenth Month." *Caught Between Coasts* (Clover Valley Press, 2018).

"The Effect of Sleeping Children." *Dust&Fire*, 1993.

"The Physician Attends a Poetry Reading." *Poets to Come: A Poetry Anthology* (Local Gems Press, 2019).

"The Plot against Juhannus Juhlat." *Trail Guide* (Calyx Press, 2008).

"Trilliums." *Wisconsin Poets' Calendar*, 2009.

"Valentine's Day." *Portage Magazine*, Spring 2017.

"Voyageurs." *A Is for Apostle Islands* (Poetry Harbor, 2021).

"White Crosses." *Fog and Woodsmoke* (Lost Hills Books, 2010).

"Whole Foods Checkout on Mother's Day." *Son of Norway* (Poetry Harbor, 2022).

"Winter Hike." *The Bottom Line*, 2019.

"Zenith City All Dressed Up." *The Thunderbird Review*, 2023.

ABOUT THE AUTHOR

Jan Chronister has been writing poetry for almost sixty years. Her work appears in a variety of journals and anthologies. Jan has won awards from Lake Superior Writers (Duluth), the Tallgrass Writers Guild (Indiana), Highland Park Poetry (Illinois), the Emberlight Festival (Michigan), the Wisconsin Fellowship of Poets, and the League of Minnesota Poets.

Jan's first chapbook *Target Practice* was published by Parallel Press at the University of Wisconsin in 2009. *Casualties*, a chapbook of Holocaust poems, was published in 2017. Her first full-length collection *Caught between Coasts* was released by Clover Valley Press (Duluth) in 2018 and recognized as an Outstanding Book in Poetry by the Wisconsin Library Association (WLA.) A third chapbook, *Bird Religion*, came out in 2019 and was awarded an Honorable Mention in the Wisconsin Fellowship of Poets chapbook contest.

Jan's second full-length collection titled *Decennia*, published in 2020 by Truth Serum Press of Australia, received the Kops-Fetherling Award for Poetry. *Distanced: Poems from the Pandemic*, Jan's fourth chapbook, was written to document the months of February through November 2020. It was recognized as an Outstanding Book in Poetry by the WLA. *Heartsick*, Jan's fifth chapbook, contains poems reflecting events in the poet's life from 2021. In 2022 Jan published a chapbook dedicated to her father titled *Son of Norway*. *Flight Patterns* (2022) is her seventh chapbook and third in what has become an annual series.

Zenith City & Beyond explores the beauty and reality of life near Lake Superior. Jan has lived and worked in Duluth off and on for over forty years, including fifteen years at the *Duluth News Tribune*.

Jan earned a degree in English from the University of Wisconsin-Milwaukee and a Masters in Education from the University of Minnesota-Duluth. She was an instructor for Viterbo University, the University of Wisconsin-Superior, Northwood Technical College, and Lac Courtes Oreilles Ojibwe College. Jan completed her teaching career with ten years at Fond du Lac Tribal and Community College, where she founded *The Thunderbird Review*.

Now retired, Jan has turned her attention to her own writing as well as publishing books for fellow poets. She and her husband of fifty-plus years tend a multitude of vegetable and flower gardens near Maple, Wisconsin.

Made in the USA
Columbia, SC
30 November 2023